THE FRENCH REVOLUTION

© Aladdin Books Ltd 1989

Designed and produced by
Aladdin Books Ltd
70 Old Compton Street
London W1V 5PA

First published in
Great Britain in 1989 by
Franklin Watts Ltd
12a Golden Square
London W1R 4BA

ISBN 0 86313 929 9

Printed in Belgium

Back cover: A painting of the guillotining of the revolutionary leader St Just.

Design	David West Children's Book Design
Editor	Catherine Bradley
Picture research	Cecilia Weston-Baker
Illustrator	Gerald Wood
Map	Aziz Khan

The author, Margaret Mulvihill, was born in Ireland and lives in London. She is the author of numerous articles for history magazines and books as well as two novels and a biography.

Contents

HISTORY HIGHLIGHTS

THE FRENCH REVOLUTION

GLOUCESTER PRESS
London · New York · Toronto · Sydney

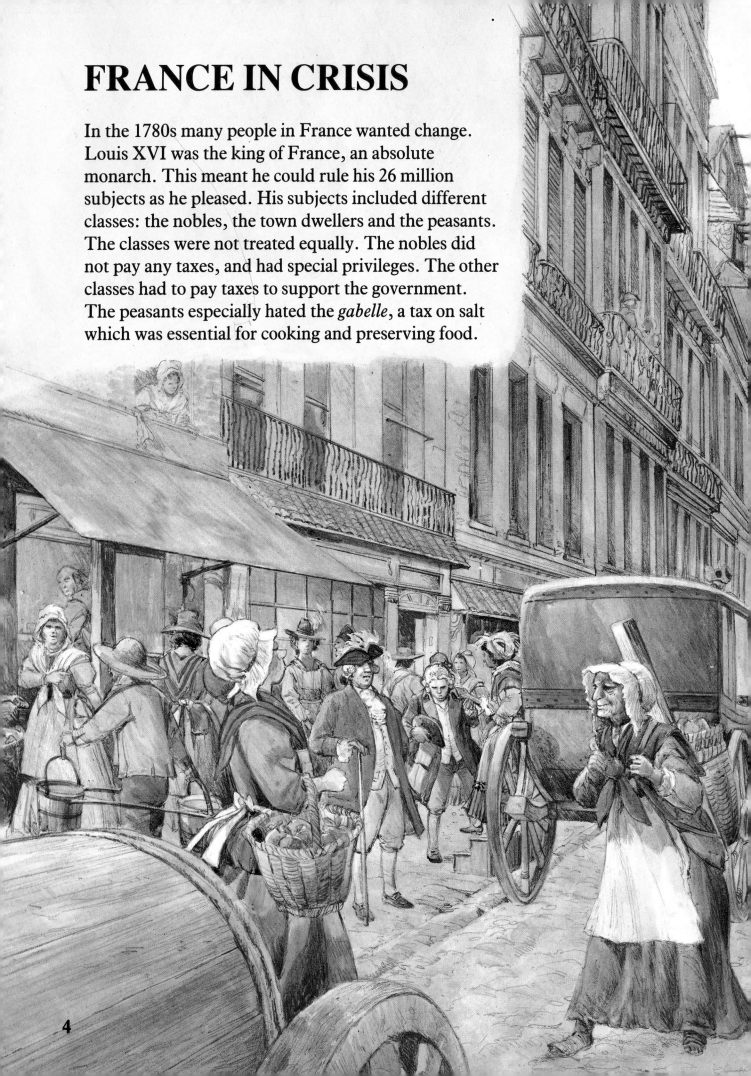

FRANCE IN CRISIS

In the 1780s many people in France wanted change. Louis XVI was the king of France, an absolute monarch. This meant he could rule his 26 million subjects as he pleased. His subjects included different classes: the nobles, the town dwellers and the peasants. The classes were not treated equally. The nobles did not pay any taxes, and had special privileges. The other classes had to pay taxes to support the government. The peasants especially hated the *gabelle*, a tax on salt which was essential for cooking and preserving food.

4

In the towns, the bourgeoisie (gentlemen) were business people or professionals. Only nobles could get high positions in government, the army and the church. The middle classes resented this. Poor townsfolk were sometimes known as *sans culottes* (without breeches) because of their loose trousers. They were often craftsmen or apprentices.

There were many problems in France. The peasants who worked the nobles' land starved when there was a bad harvest. They had to pay money to the church and had feudal obligations to their lords. They had to do unpaid work for their lords and pay other charges.

In the towns, the middle classes – lawyers, doctors, teachers and traders – were better off but they resented paying taxes. Unlike the English king, the French king did not have to consult an elected group (known as parliament) representing the middle class in order to raise taxes. Many also supported the new democracy in North America. Few were surprised when the revolution broke out in France in 1789.

PEASANT GRIEVANCES

There were many feudal obligations which the peasants resented. Every year they had to do three or more days of work on roads, bridges and waterways. The lords often controlled the wine presses, mills and ovens which peasants had to use to make wine, flour and bread. Peasants could not fish in rivers without paying the lord.

Parisians attacked the Bastille because it represented the king's power. In fact there were only a few prisoners inside – mainly forgers and lunatics. Although some soldiers were involved, most of those who attacked the Bastille were *sans culottes* from nearby – woodworkers, locksmiths and winesellers. The prison was totally demolished after the attack.

THE TENNIS COURT OATH

Jeu de Paume (an indoor tennis court) provided the Third Estate with a meeting place. There they swore to continue to meet until the king recognized them as a parliament. In fact Louis was reluctant to send soldiers against them. This dramatic moment was recreated by the painter Jacques Louis David. He painted many of the important events of the French Revolution.

THE REVOLUTION BEGINS

In 1788 a disastrous harvest led to starvation in the countryside. At the same time the king was nearly bankrupt and he needed to raise more taxes. The king called the Estates General, the body which decided new taxes. It had not met since 1614 and consisted of representatives from the three estates or groups – the first was the church, the second the nobles and the third everyone else but mainly the middle classes.

The Third Estate forced Louis to recognize it as a parliament, the National Assembly. It immediately began to discuss a new kind of government, where the king had less power. The king ordered his troops to keep the peace in Paris. On 14 July 1789 a crowd stormed the prison fortress, known as the Bastille.

THE FAILURE OF THE KING

The storming of the Bastille led to similar attacks all over France. Peasants attacked noble castles. The National Assembly backed up these actions. It also declared that all men were free and equal and that everyone would have to pay taxes. Supporters of the revolution cried "Liberty, Fraternity and Equality".

The revolt in the countryside meant the price of bread increased dramatically. People in Paris were hungry. The king remained in his palace outside Paris at Versailles. Many people thought he could improve life for ordinary people if he lived nearer the people. On the morning of 5 October 1789 a huge crowd marched to Versailles to see the king. A young woman told the king how hungry people were. That night the crowd killed some royal guards and Louis realised that he had to do what the people wanted. He returned to Paris and lived in the Tuileries Palace. Soon afterwards he had to give up his power and became a figurehead.

The women of Paris marched the 20 km to Versailles in the pouring rain. A few men accompanied them. They arrived cold and drenched. After seeing the king, the women escorted the royal family back to Paris, chanting "We are bringing the baker, the baker's wife and the baker's apprentice. They will bring us bread."

THE FLIGHT TO VARENNES

After his return to Paris, Louis tried to get his powerful friends abroad to raise armies against the revolution. The queen's brother was the emperor of Austria. In June 1791 Louis realised that his life might be in danger and organised an escape. The royal family stole out of Paris in an enormous coach. At Varennes, near France's border, patriotic citizens ended the escape.

THE REVOLUTIONARY PARLIAMENT

In 1791 the National Assembly became the Legislative Assembly. This meant it could now pass laws and decide how France should be ruled. The assembly was made up of deputies who were elected by well-off tax payers. The peasants and workers were not represented in the parliament.

During debates each deputy voted according to his own ideas. Some voted as a group. The two most important groups were the Girondins and the Jacobins. The Girondins were deputies from the provinces who thought that the revolution should be spread to other countries. They were in favour of war against countries who helped royalist armies. The Jacobins were against war and preferred a programme of reforms at home.

Since the assembly was in Paris it came under pressure from local people. On several occasions a crowd of *sans culottes* broke in and used violence to influence the assembly's decision.

The Legislative Assembly met in an old riding school, called the Manège. The most radical deputies sat on the highest seats on the left. On the right sat those who supported the king. Our terms "left" and "right" come from the seating pattern of the French revolutionary parliament.

Lafayette

Mme Roland

Talleyrand

Marat

Robespierre

Danton

Mirabeau

Olympe de Gouges

Early leaders of the revolution included Talleyrand, a bishop, Lafayette and Mirabeau, both nobles. Mme Roland was a Girondin. Danton and Robespierre were both lawyers and led rival groups. Marat was a journalist and Olympe de Gouges was a writer.

THE JACOBINS CLUB

This cartoon shows a debate taking place at the Jacobins Club. The club was named after the convent in Paris which was its headquarters. It had branches all over France and published an influential newspaper. The Jacobin deputies were more organised than other groups because they debated things in advance. Robespierre was a leading Jacobin. Danton was the leader of another club. It was called the Cordeliers and, unlike the others, allowed women to speak.

PARIS

In April 1792 France declared war on Austria and Prussia. Austrian and Prussian troops were trying to restore the King's power. The citizens of Paris, who took part in the major events of the revolution, realised they would suffer most if the royalist armies were successful. The revolutionary committee that ruled Paris, known as the Commune, put pressure on the deputies and campaigned against the king.

In September 1792 the city panicked at the news that royalist troops had broken through France's border at Verdun. Rumours spread that prisoners were about to be released and murder the citizens of Paris. Crazed with fear, a mob broke into the prisons and butchered the inmates. About 1,200 people were massacred. The deputies did nothing to stop the so-called September Massacres. Many people blamed the journalist Marat for writing articles which created an atmosphere of violence and confusion.

Living in Paris during the revolution was not easy. Most Parisians lived on bread and so were always at the mercy of price rises and shortages. When the paper money introduced by the revolutionary government fell in value, farmers did not want to sell their crops. Paris went hungry again.

Key to places

 Royalist massacre

 Revolutionary massacres

 Guillotines

1 Tuileries Palace, where the king lived
2 The Louvre Palace was made into a museum
3 National Assembly
4 Jacobins Club

5 Cordelier Club
6 Bastille, the king's prison
7 Champ de Mars, used for festivals
8 Hotel de Ville, town hall
9 Invalides, army barracks

THE EXECUTION OF THE KING

Louis XVI and his wife, Marie-Antoinette, wanted the foreign armies to succeed and restore his power. When news came through that the revolutionary armies had defeated the invading forces at Valmy in September 1792, things looked bad for Louis. On the same day France was declared a republic and Louis became plain Citizen Capet. The country was to be governed by the National Convention made up of elected deputies.

Louis XVI was a simple man whose favourite hobby was hunting. He did not fully understand events and appeared unable to make decisions and follow other people's advice. At his trial it was proved that he had been plotting against the revolution. He was guillotined in January 1793. Eight months later the queen was tried and followed him to the scaffold.

A large crowd gathered to watch the king's execution. Throughout his ordeal, Louis XVI remained dignified but his last words were drowned out by the roll of a drum.

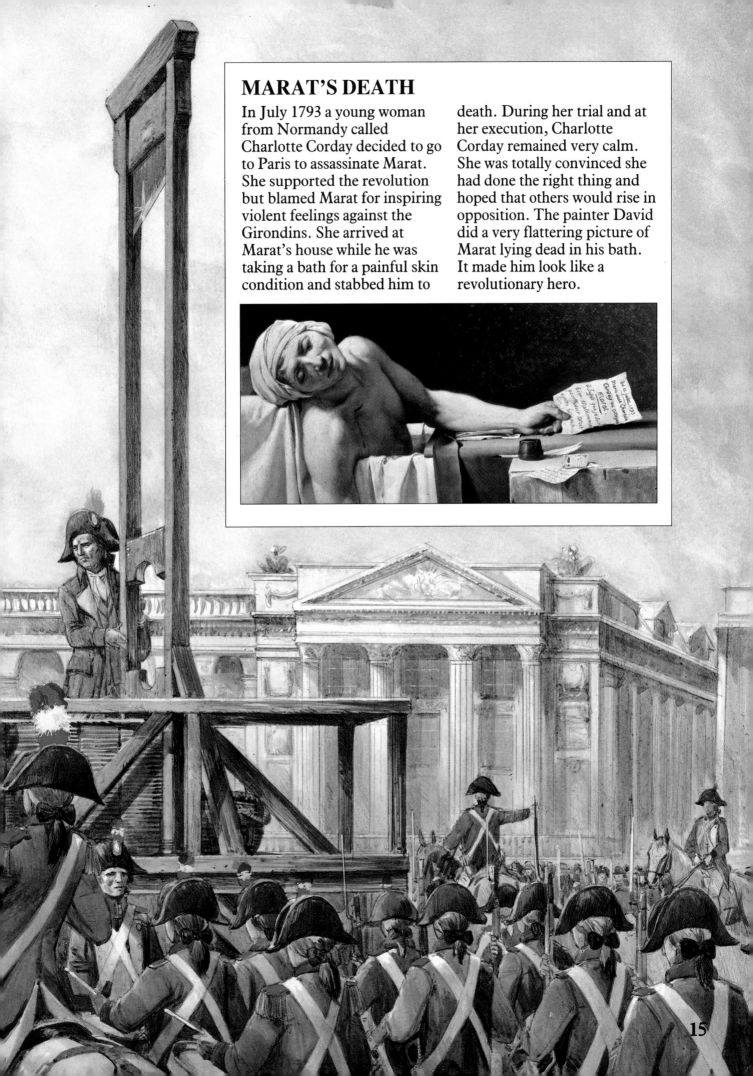

MARAT'S DEATH

In July 1793 a young woman from Normandy called Charlotte Corday decided to go to Paris to assassinate Marat. She supported the revolution but blamed Marat for inspiring violent feelings against the Girondins. She arrived at Marat's house while he was taking a bath for a painful skin condition and stabbed him to death. During her trial and at her execution, Charlotte Corday remained very calm. She was totally convinced she had done the right thing and hoped that others would rise in opposition. The painter David did a very flattering picture of Marat lying dead in his bath. It made him look like a revolutionary hero.

THE TERROR

Within months of the king's execution France was threatened on all sides by Austrian, Prussian, English and Dutch armies. In Toulon royalist rebels had handed the port over to the British. There was also civil war in several regions. In the Vendée the peasants had revolted against the revolution. The revolutionary government led by the Jacobins feared that the revolution would be overturned so a Committee of Public Safety was appointed. Anyone who was not loyal to the revolution faced arrest. Thousands were arrested, tried and executed.

This became known as the Terror and lasted from the summer of 1793 to the summer of 1794. Its extent varied from region to region. In Paris 2,639 people were guillotined and in Vendée and Lyons there were mass executions. Altogether an estimated 40,000 "enemies of the revolution" perished. Most of them were ordinary people rather than aristocrats.

At first the guillotine seemed to be a benefit of the revolution. Death by guillotine took 30 seconds and was more humane than the older methods, such as drawing and quartering or torture. But it soon symbolised the Terror. Parisian victims of the Terror had to ride in open carts (tumbrels) to the guillotine.

MADAME TUSSAUD

She was famous for making wax models and took over her uncle's business in 1794. During the Terror she was forced to make death masks from the heads of victims of the guillotine – sometimes those of people she had known. She took her collection of wax models abroad on tours of Britain and Ireland before settling in London.

CANCELLED – 9 FEB 2024

THE REVOLUTIONARY ARMY

With the revolution under threat, the Committee of Public Safety decided to raise a new army. All single men between the ages of 18 and 25 had to join up. This meant the Republic recruited some 750,000 men – one experienced man for two recruits.

By the spring of 1794 the revolutionary armies were succeeding. Vendée was in revolutionary hands, the British had been repelled at sea and royalist forces had been defeated at the Battle of Fleurus.

The revolutionary army was successful because it drew on talented people. It was now possible for men without wealth or connections to rise to important positions in the army. Carnot, who helped to organise the war effort, had been unable to get promotion in the king's army because he was not a noble. In 1793 a 24-year-old Corsican, called Napoleon Bonaparte, pushed back an Anglo-British fleet at Toulon. The military successes gave the revolutionary generals great confidence. They became an important political force.

The defence of France and the revolution depended on recruits. They were successful in battle because of their great numbers and their enthusiasm for fighting for their country. This more than made up for their lack of fighting experience.

18

LA MARSEILLAISE

The French national anthem was composed one night by a soldier named Claude Rouget de Lisle. He felt the revolutionary army needed a special marching song. It was sung with such gusto by volunteers from Marseilles on their march to Paris that it became known as the Marseillaise. In 1795 it was adopted as the national anthem.

THE REPUBLIC OF VIRTUE

The republic allowed freedom of religion. Jews and Anabaptists, for example, had the same rights as everyone else. However, during the Terror many people in Paris were very anti-Christian. Robespierre did not approve. He thought the revolution should inspire people to behave well. To encourage this "Republic of Virtue" he started the worship of the "Supreme Being", which was almost a state religion.

In June 1794 the Festival of the Supreme Being was celebrated in Paris and all over France. Robespierre set fire to a statue "Atheism" in the Tuileries Gardens and out of its ashes "Wisdom" was born. A great procession marched to the Champ de Mars, where revolutionary leaders made speeches and everyone sung hymns. Draped in velvet, the guillotine took a holiday for the festival, but it was back at its grim work next day. Festivals were held throughout France but the state religion did not become popular.

The festival of the Supreme Being was stage-managed and designed by the painter David. Rocks, trees, flowers and natural things were thought to go with democracy, in contrast with the artificial splendour of royal ceremonies. Papier mâché mountains were created in the Champ de Mars.

REVOLUTIONARY CALENDAR

In October 1793 a new calendar was adopted. France had a 10-day week with one day of rest. All the months were renamed so in the summer Thermidor meant heat, in December Nivôse meant snow and in March Germinal meant things were in bud. The calendar was put into effect in Year 2 because it was dated back to 22 September 1792, the first day of the Republic. Officials used the calendar but few others did.

Old calendar	New name	Meaning (month of)
22 Sept-21 Oct	Vendémiaire	Grape harvest
22 Oct-20 Nov	Brumaire	Mist
21 Nov-20 Dec	Frimaire	Frost
21 Dec-19 Jan	Nivôse	Snow
20 Jan-18 Feb	Pluviôse	Rain
19 Feb-20 March	Ventôse	Winds
21 March-19 April	Germinal	Budding
20 April-19 May	Floréal	Flowers
20 May-18 June	Prairial	Meadows
19 June-18 July	Messidor	Harvesting
19 July-17 Aug	Thermidor	Heat
18 Aug-16 Sept	Fructidor	Fruits

THE FALL OF ROBESPIERRE

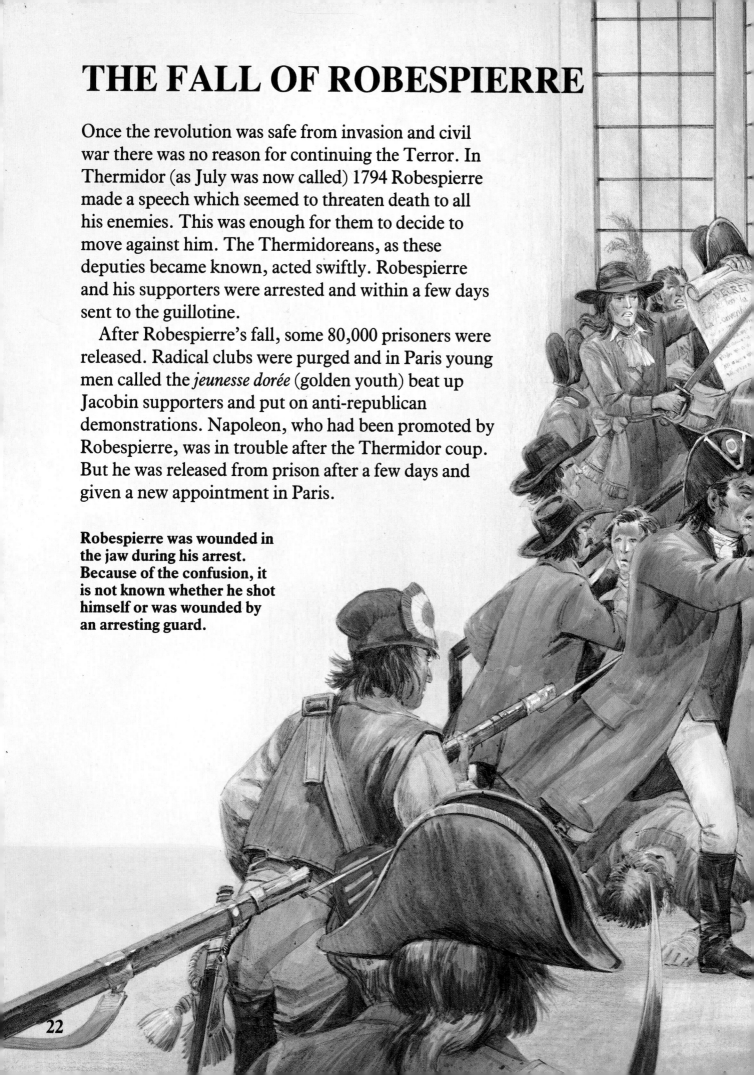

Once the revolution was safe from invasion and civil war there was no reason for continuing the Terror. In Thermidor (as July was now called) 1794 Robespierre made a speech which seemed to threaten death to all his enemies. This was enough for them to decide to move against him. The Thermidoreans, as these deputies became known, acted swiftly. Robespierre and his supporters were arrested and within a few days sent to the guillotine.

After Robespierre's fall, some 80,000 prisoners were released. Radical clubs were purged and in Paris young men called the *jeunesse dorée* (golden youth) beat up Jacobin supporters and put on anti-republican demonstrations. Napoleon, who had been promoted by Robespierre, was in trouble after the Thermidor coup. But he was released from prison after a few days and given a new appointment in Paris.

Robespierre was wounded in the jaw during his arrest. Because of the confusion, it is not known whether he shot himself or was wounded by an arresting guard.

SAINT JUST

Saint Just looked the image of a revolutionary. He refused to wear the wigs usually worn by gentlemen. He was only 21 when the revolution started and became the youngest deputy to be elected. He was a keen supporter of Robespierre and was guillotined during the Thermidor coup.

THE DIRECTORY

The Thermidoreans became very unpopular. They had been united in their fear of Robespierre but once in power they found it difficult to agree with each other. A new form of government was set up. Five deputy "Directors" were named to run France but before the Directory could take power, Paris rose up. A crowd of 20,000 assembled but Napoleon Bonaparte used guns to disperse the riot. He shrugged off the incident which became known as the "whiff of grapeshot".

The Directory lurched from one crisis to another. Many government officials were corrupt and took bribes – the country was in chaos. France had made peace with Prussia and Holland but was still fighting Austria on land and Britain at sea. Paul Barras, a leading Director, was impressed by Bonaparte's abilities and gave him a new post. He was to be commander of the force sent to conquer Italy, which was then part of the Austrian Empire.

After the fall of Robespierre, Paris became like a non-stop party. Food was plentiful for those who could afford it and luxurious clothes were in fashion again. At Bals des victimes (victims' balls), the relatives of the guillotined would wear a thin band of red ribbon round their necks.

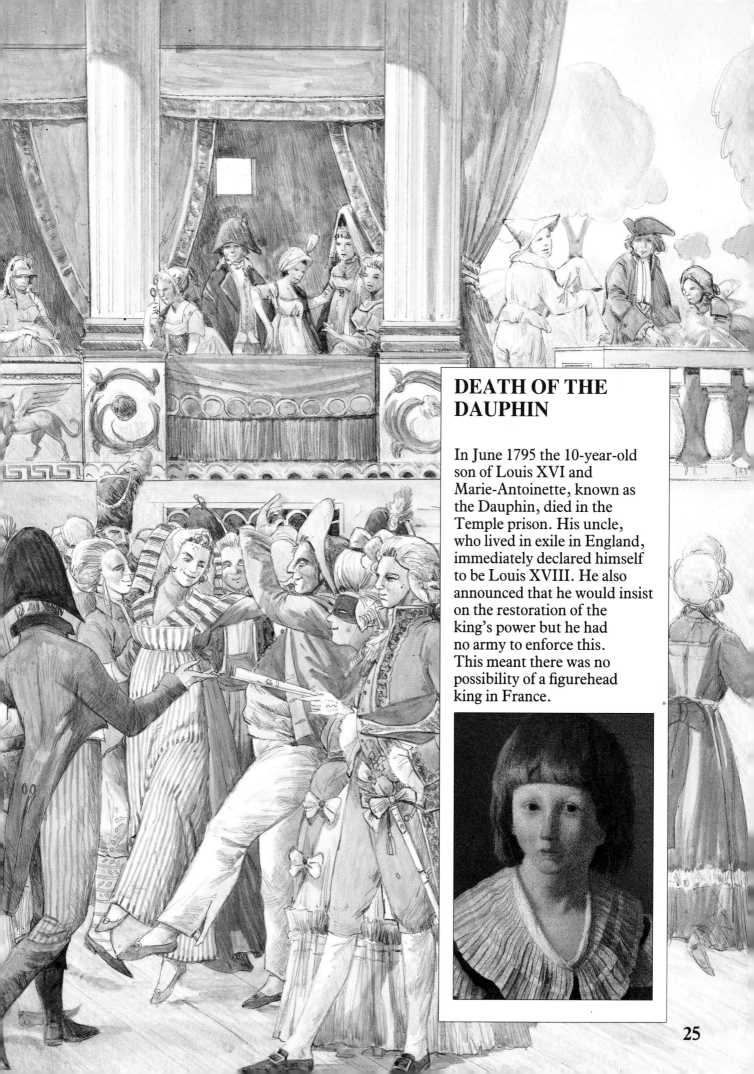

DEATH OF THE DAUPHIN

In June 1795 the 10-year-old son of Louis XVI and Marie-Antoinette, known as the Dauphin, died in the Temple prison. His uncle, who lived in exile in England, immediately declared himself to be Louis XVIII. He also announced that he would insist on the restoration of the king's power but he had no army to enforce this. This meant there was no possibility of a figurehead king in France.

THE RISE OF NAPOLEON

Napoleon's armies scored many victories in Italy and he became France's most important military figure. In Brumaire (November) 1799 Napoleon decided to seize power but it did not go smoothly. He had to threaten the politicians with his troops before they agreed to appoint him one of three Consuls.

After eight years the revolution was finally over. It had achieved much. The old feudal system had been overturned and a king would never have the same power to rule France. Many changes remain. The church never had the same power over people's lives. But the first attempt to create a government which gave people power to decide who should rule had failed. A national vote was organised which confirmed Napoleon's position as First Consul and he moved into the Tuileries Palace. Later in 1804 Napoleon crowned himself "Emperor of the French". The title was important. People were still suspicious of royalty so Napoleon could not be called king.

Napoleon thought he would be able to seize power quite easily. It took longer than he thought. The politicians voted against him so Napoleon ordered his troops to chase them from the hall. A small number of deputies were rounded up and they appointed Napoleon one of the three consuls.

JOSEPHINE

Joséphine de Beauharnais was Napoleon's wife. She was very glamorous and was important in the social world of the Directory, before she married Napoleon. Her first husband had been a revolutionary aristocrat who had signed the king's death warrant. He was guillotined a few days before the fall of Robespierre. After Napoleon crowned himself as emperor, he crowned Joséphine as empress. Before the revolution, it would have been unthinkable that a soldier would have become the ruler of France.

DEMOCRACY IS CONTAGIOUS

The French Revolution was a decisive moment in history. The revolutionary cry of "Liberty, Fraternity and Equality" was heard all over Europe and kings and dukes were afraid they would lose everything. One of the remarkable things about the revolution was that everything happened very quickly. The storming of the Bastille brought the king down. The 9 Thermidor 1794 saw the fall of Robespierre.

Many European cities rose up in 1848. By that time the spread of new factories and the growth of towns had changed traditional ways of life. In Germany, Italy, Hungary and Bohemia (present-day Czechoslovakia) the French Revolution inspired the struggle for independence. The old rulers – the Habsburg emperor, the pope, the kings of France and Prussia – fled from their palaces. In that same year Karl Marx and Friedrich Engels published the *Communist Manifesto*. This pamphlet was to have worldwide impact. Marx had studied the French Revolution and his ideas influenced the Russian Revolution in 1917.

Sainte Dominique (modern Haiti) in the Caribbean was a French colony. It was notorious for the ill treatment of its black slaves. In 1791 the slaves of Sainte Dominique were encouraged by the fall of the king to fight for their own freedom. Their leader was Toussaint L'Ouverture, a former slave. In 1794 France abolished slavery and Toussaint reunited with France. However Napoleon was keen to regain the profits from slavery and sent a naval force to Haiti. Toussaint was captured and died in prison in 1803.

THE EMPEROR

The composer Beethoven saw Napoleon as the champion of liberty and he intended to dedicate his Third Symphony to him. But when he heard of Napoleon's coronation as emperor, he crossed out Bonaparte's name on his manuscript with great force. Beethoven raged "He will become a tyrant." Even so the symphony is known as "The Emperor".

DATE CHARTS

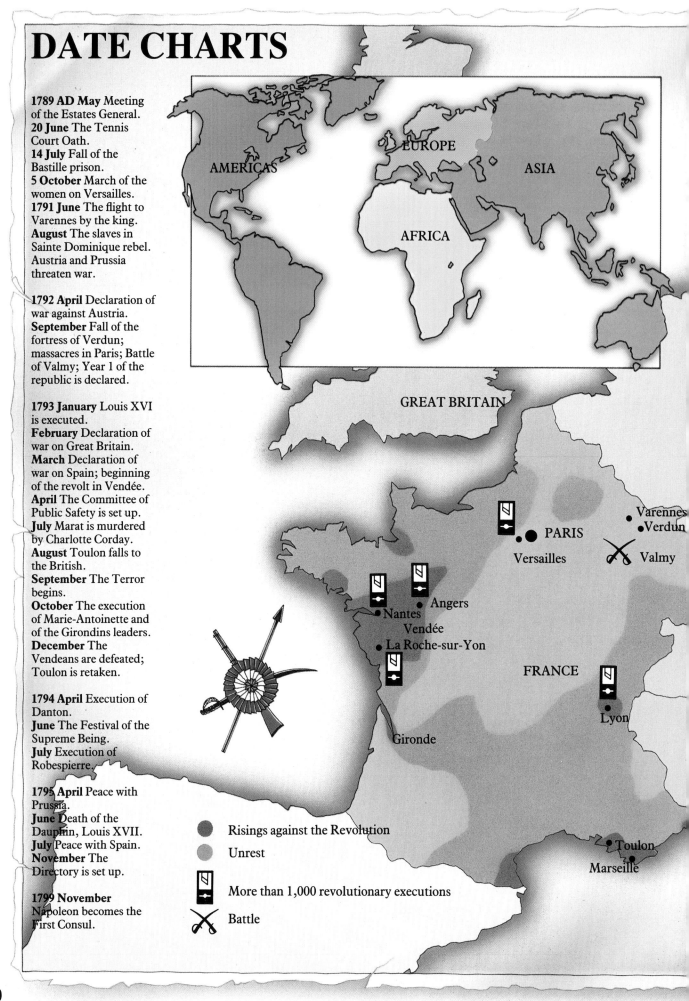

1789 AD May Meeting of the Estates General.
20 June The Tennis Court Oath.
14 July Fall of the Bastille prison.
5 October March of the women on Versailles.
1791 June The flight to Varennes by the king.
August The slaves in Sainte Dominique rebel. Austria and Prussia threaten war.

1792 April Declaration of war against Austria.
September Fall of the fortress of Verdun; massacres in Paris; Battle of Valmy; Year 1 of the republic is declared.

1793 January Louis XVI is executed.
February Declaration of war on Great Britain.
March Declaration of war on Spain; beginning of the revolt in Vendée.
April The Committee of Public Safety is set up.
July Marat is murdered by Charlotte Corday.
August Toulon falls to the British.
September The Terror begins.
October The execution of Marie-Antoinette and of the Girondins leaders.
December The Vendeans are defeated; Toulon is retaken.

1794 April Execution of Danton.
June The Festival of the Supreme Being.
July Execution of Robespierre.

1795 April Peace with Prussia.
June Death of the Dauphin, Louis XVII.
July Peace with Spain.
November The Directory is set up.

1799 November Napoleon becomes the First Consul.

EUROPE

AMERICAS

ASIA

AFRICA

GREAT BRITAIN

Varennes
Verdun
PARIS
Versailles
Valmy
Angers
Nantes
Vendée
La Roche-sur-Yon
FRANCE
Lyon
Gironde
Toulon
Marseille

Risings against the Revolution
Unrest
More than 1,000 revolutionary executions
Battle

AFRICA	ASIA	AMERICA	EUROPE
	1750 AD China conquers Tibet.		**1762 AD** Catherine the Great becomes the Czarina of Russia.
	1761-90 AD Rise of Sikh power in India.		
1775 AD The Masai expand in East Africa, reaching the Ngong.		**1773 AD** Boston Tea Party.	**1772** Poland is divided between Prussia, Austria and Russia.
		1776 American Declaration of Independence.	**1781** Joseph II of Austria abolishes serfdom and introduces religious toleration.
1787 The British establish a colony in Sierra Leone, West Africa.	**1787** Famines and food riots in Japan.		
		1791 Slave revolt in Haiti led by Toussaint L'Ouverture.	**1789** French Revolution begins.
			1793 Execution of Louis XVI.
	1796 The British take Ceylon from the Dutch.		**1794** Fall of Robespierre.
1798-99 Napoleon invades Egypt.			**1799** Napoleon becomes the First Consul.
			1800 Union of Britain and Ireland.
			1804 Napoleon becomes Emperor.
1807 The slave trade is abolished within the British Empire.			**1805** Battle of Trafalgar, Britain defeats France at sea.
1810 Zulu empire founded in southern Africa: many peoples driven north.			**1812** Napoleon leads the retreat from Moscow.
			1814 Napoleon abdicates; Louis XVIII becomes king of France.
		1816 Argentina receives independence from Spain.	**1815** Napoleon escapes from Elbe; French armies are defeated at Waterloo.
	1819 Singapore set up by Stanley Raffles.		
		1822 Great Colombia achieves independence from Spain; Brazil declares independence from Portugal.	**1820** Revolutions in Spain and Portugal.
			1829 Greece wins independence.
	1825-30 Java War: Indonesians revolt against the Dutch.	**1830** Great Colombia breaks up: Colombia, Ecuador and Venezuela become independent.	**1830** Louis-Philippe becomes the citizen king of France following the July Revolution.
1828 Death of Chaka, Zulu emperor.			
1835-37 Great Trek of Boers from British South African Territory.	**1831-40** Syria and Lebanon are occupied by Egypt.		
	1839 First Afghan War.	**1840** Canada becomes a Dominion.	**1837** Queen Victoria becomes queen of England.
1844 War between France and Morocco.	**1842** Hong Kong acquired by Britain from China.		
1847 Liberia becomes independent.		**1848** The California Gold Rush takes place.	**1848** Year of revolutions in Europe.

INDEX

Photographic Credits
Pages 2, 14, 26 and back cover: The Mary Evans Photo Library; pages 3, 6, 8, 12, 20, 22 and 24: Lauros-Giraudon; page 16: La Bibliothèque Nationale.

PRINTED IN BELGIUM BY
proost
INTERNATIONAL BOOK PRODUCTION